Footsteps In The Snow

ISBN: 978-1-291-31940-8

For Betty Walker and Martyn Ward.

For showing me what the true meaning of strength is.

Thank You

To my Nan, Betty Walker.
Your love for me was always constant. I know you know that I love you just as much back. I will not say goodbye to you. I will see you later.

To my Dad. Martyn Ward. You make me proud every moment of every day. I am so lucky to have had you.

To the rest of my family. Mum, Adrian, Fiona, Teravis, I love you too.

To The Girls. Lou-Lets Get This! G-Get out the Jailbait!

You all inspire me more than you will ever know.

Claire and Katie O' Connor, Mark Read, Marina Fawson, Marte Bang, Rosina Carr and Ryan Tyler-Smith for just being you.

Judith Coombes and David Eccles. The English Teachers who said that one day I could do this.

Jeramiah Ambrose. For showing me how I can do this. I will promote your book (Up Syndrome) if you promote mine.
Mitchell Greasley for my cover.
Anyone else that I forgot. Insert your name and I thank you to.

Contents:

Fiona

There is something to be said for the way that I feel about you. A crazy love that I can't control. I can't try to make it rational; it is what it is.

The first time I saw you I think I fell under your spell. I had waited so long and from that first moment you were mine. Nothing could take you, nothing could ruin it. You are perfect. In the ways that you are not perfect. A stroppy little madam. A princess. A kettle kettle teapot. Everything you should be, is all part of the package.

I hear the songs that remind me of you. Whoever thought there would be anybody who's taste in music was as bad as mine?

I playback the movies that we have shared and enjoyed. The ones we have found lacking, deplored of the plot lines. The ones we put on just because the men in them were hot.

I mentally snapshot you right here. Right now. Store the memories away somewhere safe. So many pictures. So many moments. Anticipation of the many to come.

You have given so much joy. Have caused me to laugh, to cry, to make me so angry I could spit.
But also to want to wrap my arms around you and hold

you so tight.

I have wiped away your tears. I have shared your smiles. Played with your hair. Shopped for pretty dresses, and I must have them boots.

You cost me a fortune. I loved it.

You are my everything. My heart. My soul.

My baby sister.
I love you. Forever.

No Title

Stomach lurching. Throat turns dry. My body burns with anger. How can I bare to listen, when they say my Dad will die.

I can't believe the words I am hearing. How can life be so cruel. It only seems like five minutes, since he picked me up from school.

I try to think of a future. One in which you are not there. It doesn't still now seem real. You are a constant in how you care.

You show such strength of spirit. You joke to try to pull me through. Yet the cancer still eats away at you. You try to hide from me when you are blue.

I cherish every minute. Every second of John Wayne. I watch the westerns with you. And try to lock away the pain.

I do not want you to see it. I do not want to hurt you with my tears. You were always there to help me, when I had to face my fears.

Wanting to make you proud every second. I think of you each day. I am not ashamed to admit, that I am living in dread. Of when the Angels take you away

Life's Lessons Taught

Hold your head up high. Look the world in the eye. For you have nothing to be ashamed of.

Bottom in. Boobs out, and Smile. Smile at them all. In return they might just smile right back.

Give your all. But don't work too hard. Take time to rest. take care of your health. when you need it accept the help.

When happiness passes. Grab on to it. Grab on to it with both hands and you hold on tight. You may never get that chance come around again.

These are the lessons on life that you gave us. Words to hold dear, when the distance takes our breath away.

The time keeps on passing and still I can hear. Your words whispering to me. Like you are here and now.

The Absent Friend

I stop to check my phone again. I am waiting for a reply. I have learned not to expect it. Although once it was guaranteed.

How long has it been? A number of years. I'm still holding on. Trying to work out what it was that changed.

A friendship started unintentionally. A little quip there, a small joke here. To me it felt natural. It seemed it was that way to you too.

Having so much in common. That surprised even me. A doctor, A spaceship. A horror movie-or three. The music? That's debatable. A huge place we differ. But that was always ok. It made you laugh. And I too, was laughing at me.

"Laughter is the best medicine."

A wise man once said. Throughout the years I have tried to keep you laughing. I would hunt out the silliest of things.The shared jokes-of which there are many. And I have always been the one to conceed that yes mine are terrible, especially the Christmas ones. You accepted with rolled eyes, the text that said "splat".

In a world that moves faster, I struggled to keep up with you. You seemed to move forward, with eyes facing back;

A youthful pursuit revisited seemed to take it away. My importance soon faded. I became again just one of many. A face in the crowd.

I try to hide the heart that is still aching. Hold my head up high and smile, see if I could get you to catch on. I have tried telling you outright. The words just came out all wrong to me. In my head it sounded just fine.

Maybe I should have given up trying. But I still want what was there.

So I send you a message, then I stare at my phone. I don't want to be annoying.

I just want you to come home

Unrequited

To say I want you is too simple.
The brilliance of your smile blinds me.
It all makes me feel insane.
I know you do not feel this way about me, that the longing is all on the part of mine.
That is the shame within. The guilt I cannot confess to.

So for what I can get I will settle. To be as near as I can. I long to receive your message. I keep awake and dream of what could be.

I know your skies are different. Your destination residing on another shore.

It doesn't stop me longing. And hoping for hello. I lay down and say a small prayer, to the heavens looking down. That your star will keep on shining. That you are happy though, somehow.

Footsteps In The Snow

The street lamp was shining. Casting an eerie glow on the floor. With her eyes cast downwards. She knew where to go. A million times she has walked there. In a life time nothing has changed. The houses, the kerb stones. A hedge. Yes that's the wall.

Her heart it felt heavy, because nothing can stay the same. In a world that keeps changing; the same steps she replayed. Over and over. And keep turning back. Every winter it was like this. Every year she seemed to get no further. A long arduous journey. Stay focused she tells herself. Keep both feet steadily moving.

Her footsteps are slow.

Still with determination she continues. Her jaw she set tight. She knows she can get there. She has to get there. Are they all waiting? Is the light burning in welcome.

Drawing her coat tighter round her, she tries to ignore the chill. The icy wind blowing around her. Her hair felt so damp. The snow keeps falling from the sky. Not quite a blizzard, but enough to cover the ground.

How many times has she done this? Times too numerous to count.
She hopes we all notice. An acknowledgement that she is there; still trying. Still walking near. All she needs is some small thing. To carry her to where she belongs. To that place she has fixed in her mind.

But in those early hours. When she needs it the most, we are warm, safe and cosy. Inside in our homes. None of us stop, to take the time and look.

To pause for just one second;

And see the haunting imprints, of her footsteps in the snow.

The Return

Step off of a plane. You see the glass and blonde pine
ahead in the terminal before you.
The air bites your skin. The prickle of Scandinavian ice.
This is familiar. You have been there before.

Through the checks of immigration. Now so automatic.
You don't need to think. You just do. You let your
fingers wander, over the touch screen. Insert the foreign
money, and wait for the ticket to come at you. You take
it and go. To the gates to your right. On to the train. No
not train. Flytoget...

...How long has it been since that word was on your
tongue. Why had you let them slip away. Chide yourself
gently. Let yourself claim back the knowledge.

A twenty minute journey. It's soon that you are there.
The shops loom either side of you-you forgot this was a
hill. Stop here. Step there. Now wait for the tram. Not
tram. Trikk. There is another word. And penger. And
billett and the phrase that should have changed
everything. The words you did not hear.

Keep going. No. Don't stop to think. Don't let yourself
look for that face. Push back all of the memories. You
are not here to visit that place.

Focus instead on what's before you. The palace at the
top.

Karl Johans had had you longing. To walk here once again. Past the church on your right. The sign for the chocolate brand up high. It's surprising that that should still be there, and yet that it is, is just right.

The hotel you check into is as grand as you please. The room has a view. Like the suite you once stayed In. You hear the laughter echo down the years-look out of the window, hear the songs as if they're still playing. Yet the only sound that is the same, is the pounding of your heart.

You take yourself out and you wander. Just as you remembered, the thunder of the fountain dominates your senses. The question arises. One you have asked so many times before. The answer you were given makes sense. But that wasn't magical at all. In a world that was changing. The magic was needed.

Let yourself look now. You know you won't find it. But this is a habit of a lifetime and your heart fills with hope, even though its impossible. All you want is a glimpse. One moment once more. To look at a stranger and instead find the face that you are there searching for. The man with that name. He is not there. Nor will those moments be again... The smile and the glint in the eye. Long gone. Your heart still reaches back though. To the time when you thought that he. he was the one. That the here would turn into home.

Reach back a little further. Remember the music that was played. In two different languages. How different it was after the barricade. Let yourself stop now. Don't open the wounds. He could have been that one in that moment.

But he wasn't that one. And this isn't home.

Get up and be steady. Let your feet take you there. Again there is no need to think of where you are going. You know it's to the perpetual flame.

Sit by the water and look at the boats. Feel the Ffjord breeze gently kiss your hair.... Remember the warming of hands and the taste of ice cream...You can't remember the choice you made then, just that it was good. They were not always that good.

Now let yourself move forward. Quickly. It doesn't help to dwell there..you cannot change what has been...

...The passing of years slip by so quickly. In a blink of an eye it was done. The eye like a camera took pictures, and saved them forever, all there in your mind. Where it ended. That last kiss goodbye. The wave of a hand. The reluctance to let go...

...And then there was that other. The force that swept you away. This place was something you never shared with it. This you kept for yourself.

Head into a bar. Get offered a seat. Smile at the young man, with his hopes all ahead. Over the coffee you linger. Saver the moment. Let the taste fill your senses and the caffeine your veins. One of life's long addictions. One of the things that just stayed the same.

Slowly you make your way back. The the lobby of marble and carpet. Look back at the lift, see the egyptian carvings above the desk. Up and up. To the seventh floor. To the place where that statue lives.

With an experienced flourish you handle the door. A swipe of a card and your back in. Take your time in making ready..

...and close your eyes. On your final Norwegian night.

A Poem

Poetry at school they taught us. Is a majestic and honoured art form. The words on the page that seem to dance and come alive. An expressing of minds and an expressing of hearts. A way of telling stories. Of love, and life and war.
Some long and long winded, and some are short, pretty and sweet. It doesn't really matter, on the format, if on the sheet your own words dance.

The names of those who wrote them all echo down the years; the Wilfred's, the Owens, some women and the bard. They all had an abundance of talent and subjects aplenty. Others in inspiration, just used the flowers in the yard.

So I try to write a poem. Rhyming couplets aren't my thing. I just put pen to paper, and hope what comes out will make sense.

I think back to my school days. To the long haired teacher who asked of me"Who can write a poem?"

Anyone who tries it seems.

Self Freedom

I have never known anybody quite like you. That's because there is nobody like you.
You make the world light up with a smile. Yet you don't see the world smile back.
You make the balance right. Yet you always feel off kilter.
You show others compassion, love and strength. You have it for others but never for yourself.

This is your fault.

I try to give you something. To show you what I mean. The words always fall empty and barren. You know their meaning and cannot seem to apply them to your heart. It gets blocked by your head.

So stop for a second. Close your eyes and drown out the din.
Let the words sink in. Feel their meaning. Let the doubts go.

Open your eyes. See the world. Anew.

A Chance

Take my hand and lead me. I will follow where you go. Don't be afraid to reach out. This chance could change it all.

If it only lasts for a minute. Then make that minute worth while. You can't get back a happines is that's past. But you can create again.

If all this leads to falling, then I will hope to fall there too. But If it's not forever, then that is quite alright. No harm, no foul they say.

Always hold fast though. That each of our small moments, are just the tip of an iceberg, in the ocean we call life.

So let your heart be open. Let the past be gone. You can only move on forward. The future is ours to hold.

The Roadtrip

Get ready to go. Pay a little visit. Make sure you have all you need.

Faces are smiling as you all pile out. Into the sunshine, down to the car.

Adjust your seat. Strap yourself in tight. You chose the music carefully.

Off to the petrol station. Grumble at the prices. Inflation, or what?!

Cries of are we there yet? And sweets passed all round.

This one needs a stop off. With pleas of right now!

Change the cd quickly. Turn up loud the sound. Dance along to the beat.

Keep going again your getting there slowly. Point out the first road sign.

Miles pass by, with eager anticipation. You're nearly there.

The hunt for a parking space is fraught with desperation.

Pile out of the car. Clap your hands with joy. You're finally by the sea.

Another Day Closer

Why did you have to go there?
Why did you have to make me sad?
Please just stop and be calm for a moment.
Let me take a second to calm my breath.

I needed some understanding. Not you shouting because you are unwilling to comprehend. I know it's a catch situation. And our anger makes it worse.

I want to make you listen. To hear what's inside my heart. You cannot understand the fears that do not live inside my head.

Sometimes talking isn't helpful. The words just come out wrong. How can it be so empty, when the inside is so full?
Sometimes the only way is to scream. Pure fury and rage dwell within. Destruction haunts the nights.

Sleep is also lacking. There is no rest to be had. I have come to hate the night time. Resentment towards the bed. The stars that shine above, are only there to mock, and to be a reminder that hastens on tomorrow. Another day closer to the end.

I do not want the sorrow. I do not want the pain. I need the voice to quieten. So I can too think straight. There is no sense of logic. There is no reason here to find, just those left still searching for answers that do not exist

Behind The Veil

I can still hear the music playing. Feel the beating of my heart. I stood and watched you walk away. The day we parted in the park.

Smiles on both of our faces. The assurance of "I'll see you soon". Soon could not get there fast enough. So eager to be by your side.

So I hoped and waited for the next time, to make that sideward glance. To hope that you would see me. And notice my intentions.

With seemingly pure connotations, I flirted, smiled and wooed. There came one day, I chanced to hope, that the light would shine on me.

You never saw me looking. You never saw that it was you. I hid behind my veil, the face of just a friend. I watched you fall for others, my heart crushed secretly, time and time over again.

So why do I still love you? Why do I still glance that way at you. I tell myself it's just a habit.
But I still hope you'll look in my direction.

Kisses On The Breeze

Look out. Not with your eyes. Use your mind and focus.
Look hard, just let your mind go searching.

Past the trees, down to the water and beyond. Just
beyond the horizon is where I will be. Waiting there for
you. As if on a dream.

I know for you it's hurting. But I am happy now. I spend
my days here with you. You can still find your strength
in me.

Do not think of me in sorrow. Do not stand by that stone
and weep. It may not be tomorrow, but I know again we
will meet.

I know you love the summer. The warmth on your skin.
But for me I loved the autumn. When the wind, it blows
the trees.

It's not that I am not with you, it's just not me that you
can see. But when you start to close your eyes and drift
away, that is where I'll be.

I know you'll miss my kisses. Upon your cheeks they
laid.
I will still be giving you kisses. They will come to you
on the breeze.

Strap On A Smile

I'm going to strap on a smile and pretend to be strong. Hide just how much this hurts.

Don't want to inflict it on anyone else. The nights I spend awake are too hard to face. It doesn't seem like it is ever going to end. I wish that I could be what you want to me to be. I wish I could fulfil the image you have in your mind. To keep up with your expectations I will strap on a smile.

I want to make you think I am happy. I want you to think I am counting my blessings. But I am not. I am screaming. Inside but not allowed. To you I will strap on a smile.

You know me so well, but not enough to see how I am breaking. I do not want you to know, how weak I really am. That curling up seems like the only option I have inside.

I don't want you to know what a coward I am. So when we meet I will continue to strap on a smile.

Believe

Do you believe? What do you believe?Is there a higher power?
Look at the world around you. What do you see? War, hurt, anger and destruction.
Do you see the images of suffering and hold them as evil? The lack of dignity that has been stripped away..

But what of the beauty? Do you see flowers, wind on the leaves? Do you see sunlight glittering on the seas? Listen to a baby laughing away. Stop for the flowers.
Do you see the humanity in trying to help? The need for mankind to reach out its hand?

Do you believe that goodness can overcome the dark?
That the beating of your heart is a miracle in itself.
Do you believe that we are forever? That the love stays on?

Two Weeks Notice

What can you say when words fail you?
What can you say when inside is numb and screaming both?
What can you say when all there is is I love you, and I love you means nothing?
What can you say when you open your eyes and the nightmare doesn't go away?
What do you say when what you don't want to hear keeps on being said?
What do you do with a deadline that will not go away?
Where do you go when you run out of places to run?
Where do you find the strength to face the future and carry on?
What do you think when your brain goes into overdrive yet there is nothing to process?
How can you focus when all the colour is fading?
How can you think of smiling again when the joy is fleeing?
What can you do when death approaches?

What do you do with two weeks notice?

The Waiting Game

Do not sit around waiting. Watching the world go by.
The time you waste can never be returned to you.
The cost of time is dear.
Let your soul experience the joy of the day. The
sunshine and the rain are both needed to make a
rainbow.
Love and life still happen, even though you feel the pain.
Though it may be bracing, it's the bad that shows the
sweetness of all things good.

Let your mind run riot, let yourself have fun. You owe it
to yourself to cherish every minute. Think of those who
wish they could.
Do not let your worries stop you and weigh you down.
There is always someone to help carry the load.The
friends you have could surprise you. If you only let them
try.
Procrastinating will not make you mobile. And still the
time will pass. In a blink of an eye you will have missed
that chance.

Do not sit around waiting. Do not play that game. Fix
your eyes straight forward. Exhilaration in the gain.

Missed

It was good to hear your voice. The laughter in it made me smile.Stepping away from the anger, the fear and the shame. I opted for teasing you, and making light of how much I missed you. To try to take my heart off of my sleeve, and not do as I want to.

How can it be that so much time had passed? How unreal when we used to talk all of every day? Can we get back there? My stomach flutters at the thought of you and me being that way again.

How did we get here? That we are almost strangers yet know each other so well? That you know me in that way. Not yet my lover. You're more than a friend. A quasi enigma that has me baffled.

How easy was it to say that I have missed you? How strange that you should say you missed me too? Shouldn't this say something? Tell us there is a road that we should try to explore. That the line needs to be crossed.

Time is on our side, so we do not need to rush. But time can also be a thief and passes in a blink.
Has the absence shown you yet what we have been trying to say? The proof of the pudding is in the tasting.
You have to bite the apple to know its sweetness.
Do you not see the potential shared?

Fear

Have you ever felt a fear so wrenching that you cannot breathe.
A terror that I will lose you too.

I wish I could have freeze framed that moment when everything was right. So we could live there and be happy forever.

I look at the others and wonder if they feel it too. See into their eyes and read nothing but pain. This is unspeakable, so wrong. It cuts like a knife.

Taking back yesterday is impossible to do. No matter how hard you try. Praying resounds hollow, your faith falling flat. Your face on the ground. There is no going back.

I want you to hold me. Say that everything is ok. But I know it never will be. I look at your face and keep crossed my arms. Not to stop me from loving you but to protect me from harm.

Pride

I enjoyed the time we spent. Just looking at the sky. The clouds were white upon the blue.. Still tinged with that hint of grey.

Holding on to the chair. To keep you steady and anchor me to the earth. I tried to look out with your eyes. To see if I could see the world with your perspective. Is it still beautiful? To me it seems broken. As if the balance is somehow askew.

Laughing at the silly mistakes that have been made, our breaths catch.I wait for yours to keep up... Follow every one with my breaking heart. Your determination is still showing through. Your war still waging on this inevitable ending. You will not go down easily. A refusal to quit.

Try to project my pride. To make you feel all of the words I cannot say. I love you suffices where the others die on my tongue. Unable to give them life, they resound in my head. I do not want to lose you, but I know you cannot stay.

You left me far too quickly. To fast you flew away. A gentle sigh passed, and with it you were gone.

Dad

My heart was stolen in the night. You left me on a sigh.
Just a few moments passed and a lifetime looks a long
way lonely.
I had you to love. The words were spoken. Oh how you
laughed at me. As you always had.

It was me who told my brother. How my heart aches to
have to tell him so. He says I did it nicely. And that the
love was shown. I hope I did you proud.

I don't want to let you go. Even now it doesn't feel right.
I know you would be there for me. I know you would be
here to kiss us goodnight.

My heart is breaking for you. My eyes can't look forward
yet. I still need you here for me. At the end of the phone.
To be there when I fall. To pick me up when I need it.
To open the doors when I can't do it myself. To stand at
the end of the alley and protect me from the monsters.

You need to be told off. You left us here. Four blondes
and him. Who is going to tell me how I do it? And praise
me when it's done?

Who else but you could have made it that way?

Missing you is forever.

Old Friend

I thought of you today and smiled. My friend I miss you so.
It may have only been an hour but time stretches when you are gone.

The laughter keeps on coming. The tears rolling down my face. The way you come is so natural. We both belong in the here and now.

The gulf that separates us, may be an ocean wide. But that is not forever, we have time here on our side.

You know I wouldn't change you. I want to keep you whole. In the wind you are unswaying. A constant solid soldier. The battles rage around us. We just stay the same.

Food For Thought

Some situations you just cannot win. You give and you give and the return is never coming. You keep on trying because you feel that if you don't you will only lose.

Sit and think for a while. Explore all options. Dismiss them out of hand. And then think them over again. Too hard on your dreams, you lay them aside. Yet by not reaching, you can never touch the stars.

At what point do you choose, to give in and take the route that you began with? Is it at the point of no return? Or when something can be salvaged? Let yourself feel the footsteps of a new adventure.

Weigh up the costs of your indecision. It may become that they are too high. Are you playing here for gain, or are your endeavours pointless.

Who are you seeking to frustrate? Is it yourself you are battling with? Why put yourself through the torment. It's achievements are worthless.

Surly life would be easier if the focus was on what you want. Instead of what you tell yourself you don't. It may seem hard to let go of your insecurities. The only person they are hurting, is you.

Smile

Pray for a miracle. Hold your dreams tight. Do not let them go. Sit by the ocean and watch the waves lap. Lose yourself in the peace.

Take a stroll by the harbour. Down the street, in the field. Cast your eyes towards the heavens. Count the stars until your eyes are heavy with the need to sleep.

Be thankful for your blessings. No matter how small. Even the light reflected on a puddle can be enough if you let it.

Take comfort in your friendships. Let each fill you up. The vial will only remain empty if you don't turn on the tap.

Smile at strangers. Each smile is a gift. It is offered so simply and returning it can make someone's day.

Take yourself out and dance in the rain. Feel the freshness on your skin, love the chill in the air.

The snow is for watching, wrapped up warm as it falls. Then outside in the crispness. Make yourself an angel. Fill the air with your laughter. Savour the joy.

For You

You asked for something happy. Some thing full of delight. I get happy when I am with you, all the times we danced all night!

I love to go shoe shopping, then to see you standing on one foot. With a posture just like Eros, a picture of the boot you shot!

The warming liquid coursing through you, the outcome has only once been repeated, on that Island that is so green.
I long again for the weekend, and the adventures we'll have yet!

www.ingramcontent.com/pod-product-compliance
Ingram Content Group UK Ltd.
Pitfield, Milton Keynes, MK11 3LW, UK
UKHW021051270726
13967UKWH00012B/253

9 781291 319408